CW01543980

How to use the book:
This isn't something to be afraid of, step cautiously around or refuse to go near. Work your way through the pages carefully, at your own speed and try not to rush. This is a collection of my thoughts and the parts of me that make me most human. There is always light at the end of the tunnel. If you find yourself stuck in the negatives skip to The Accepting and you'll find more positives to lift you up from there onwards.

Remember, over everything, in time you'll be just fine.

Your shadow cannot leave.
You may want it to, but
because of the world's
physics it simply can't.

You can't run and hiding
keeps you out of the light.

There's The Worst Of It,
where you don't know
you can hide.
The Finding,
where you find someone
to hide you.
The Accepting,
where you notice there
is no point in hiding.
and The Living,
Where you realize the
sun is so much more
enjoyable when you're
in it.

You cannot ask the shadow
to leave and never return,
for it does not speak our
language.

But you can invite it to dance.

- Ruby-Marie

Dedicated to my coffee drinkers, my over thinkers, the people who stay up too late and the people who haven't been on a first date. To the people who mix mayonnaise with ketchup and those who struggle to get up. For my men and my women, and those in between and for the people who think they are not seen.

If we cannot
be human,
what can we be?

The worst of it.

- When you think the world is ending, and you have nowhere else to run.

- This is it right?

Some thoughts are
not meant to be repeated,

yet we find ourselves
saying things we know
we shouldn't.

Perhaps a drop in your stomach, a raise in adrenaline or the palms on your perfectly put together body start to form beads of sweat.
When you're nervous

I was trying to
embrace insecurities
I wouldn't have if the
world wasn't so goddamn
biased.

There wasn't anyone, as far as I was aware. It was just me and whatever I was given to hold by this thing called life.

Things were getting too heavy.

Like when a cloud gets too full, it just has to drop everything it holds, because not even emotionless creations can hold the weight they must.

So why do you expect us to?

Life isn't meant to harmonise like an orchestra.

Don't pretend it should.

Dear Society,

You're making people starve themselves to look like something photoshopped.

Stop it.

Can you not see, I'm drowning. I'm not asking for help because,

"be strong" they said as they watched my tears fall.

"They are only jealous" they insisted, but what was there to be jealous of.

"They aren't worth your time" I had no one else to give my time to, and I didn't need it.

I'm was still smiling, because the last thing I ever wanted was for someone else to recognize and unstitch my weaknesses.

I was just tired.

We were taught that when someone "isn't very nice" it's just because they are jealous.

By telling us that, you're making us into the people who are 'just jealous'

Teach me that some people were raised in an environment that made them not very nice.

Pillows muffle cries,
but sometimes you
need a person to
be your pillow.

My empty skin was
not an invitation for you
to make it ugly.

Your heart breaks for yourself when you realise that you need to be saved.

But have convinced yourself you aren't worth the lifeboat.

You had me convinced that I was the problem.

You had me convinced that I was worthless.

You had me convinced I deserved this pain.

You had me convinced I was useless.

You had me convinced I was alone.

You had me convinced I was broken.

You had me convinced that I was ugly.

You had me convinced that I was annoying.

You had me convinced that I was a joke.

You had me convinced I wasn't worth the time.

You had me convinced I wasn't worth the effort.

You had me convinced no one would love me.

You had me convinced.

Manipulated

The mirror was never my best friend. It lied to me, told me things I didn't want to hear. It slipped false information into my heart and made me believe I shouldn't look like this.

> Your hips shouldn't be that wide.
> Your waist should be thinner.
> Where's your thigh gap.
> Your body doesn't curve smoothly.
> Your stomach isn't flat.

Motivation is your
best friend when you
have it,

and your worst enemy
when you don't.

And just like motivation, time is your best friend and your worst enemy.

You begin to believe you're losing touch with
the people you're around because you missed
that joke, or someone shot you a smile and
you didn't return it, you're just losing.

You end up feeling like
the entire world is
shooting arrows through
your digestive system,
head and heart.

Don't look at me
like I asked to
feel broken.

I would sit on my bed and cry, weeping and begging for my sanity. It seemed to have grown legs and run away.

We didn't ask for this. We didn't ask for our grades to be ruined, we didn't ask to be depressed, anxiety filled, breaking down from the inside out. We didn't ask to be born. I know I don't speak for all of us, because I'm sure some of us are living their best life, finally learnt to love themselves, they can look in the mirror and say "Hey, I did a good job today" but trust me when I say I know more of us can't.

Sometimes rather
than pitying me
I wish someone
told me to
open
my mouth
rather than
shut it.

I wanted it to stop.

I had so much to live for, so much. My family, my friends, my dogs.

The sunrises, the sunsets, the ice cream and the chocolate.

The countries, continents and capitals I'd never seen before.

The people who needed me more than I need myself.

Yet I still didn't want to be here.

I found myself
repeating a word
that was never needed
nor wanted in the
situation

I'm sorry

Why I wasn't there
does not concern you.

So please do not ask,
I refuse to let you
make my pain into
a joke.

I didn't take 5 days out of my education just because 'I didn't feel like it', I took 5 days out of my education because I couldn't leave the house without it feeling like my lungs were being put through a meat grinder.

When you lose all care for yourself and your wellbeing, is when you truly begin to believe that your time is up.

I was never trying to copy, I just couldn't find myself in time. I had to be someone. So I chose to be you for a while.

Your pain doesn't show up with an axe and poison. It appears as whatever you thought you loved the most.

Stop dragging yourself
down a sandpaper slide
and pretending it's
slippery.

- A childhood friend who saved me

Us humans like to be ambitious
and with ambition
comes the slow grinding away
of your hope for yourself.

You made me who
I am today,

I may hate you,
but you built
me.

The finding.

- There will always be someone out there to make life easier, you just have to be willing to look.

- Don't over use your new found 'saviour' they are human too.

- An overthinker's reason to worry.

It might just have
been you,

that made me
realise life was
worth living.

You became part of my morning routine, as if you were always meant to be there.

A gap was left that you slotted yourself into and suddenly my puzzle was one more piece closer to being complete.

You don't remind me of my past.

That's what I like most

The act of mistaking
want for need,
is a dangerous one
at that.

You may want something, or someone, more than you can possibly describe to anyone or yourself.

But do not fall into the trap of convincing yourself you need someone to breathe.

Laugh with me like
it's the purge and
we just stole 8
bags of sweets.

I need you

You filled up my craving
for connection like an
empty flower pot
overflows when the
rain pours.

How did you find me in a maze that was custom made?

I may have been looking for you, all this time.
My body will do odd things, search for people
and objects whilst I'm not trying to and then
when they appear it's like a surprise gift.

I'm doing myself favours.

I may have been looking for something else
too, but I'm not sure what. Perhaps my urge to
write is a reflection of spilling my feelings onto
a page.

I'm helping myself

I may have been convinced I was helpless, but
there's always help to be found, you attract
the same energy you give out, and sometimes
it takes faking that energy to get what you
want.

The mirror still isn't my friend

But you are.

I'm okay right?

Humans aren't built to fit together. Although we are not all exactly the same, we all have the same blueprint. 2 arms, 2 legs, a head, torso, hips, you get the idea. Think of it like jigsaw pieces, the parts that fit together are very different, if you had two pieces that were exactly the same in most cases you would find that they don't fit together. It's like our limbs really. Think of us like puzzle pieces, we aren't meant to fit together. That is why we are all slightly different, so when we long for it, the right person will always end up slotting with us so perfectly.

Sometimes though, the wrong person can be mistaken for the right one, then we force ourselves to fit together, eventually, like puzzle pieces you could get it to work, but it would be so uncomfortable.

But you convince yourself this is how it's meant to feel.

- *The uncomfortable act of human connection*

Hug me like
a corset would hug
a wealthy woman from the
1600's waist.

You will never feel the same way about two different people. The feeling will always be slightly different.

Find all the people who fire at the part of you that makes you laugh, each of them shooting a different arrow.

I want to organise
things that,

aren't meant to
be organised.

You cannot beg for help all of the time, the right person will offer.

Begging for help from the wrong person is like skydiving without a parachute.

When I cannot hold up myself anymore, you'll be there to hold me up won't you?

Won't you?

You can't start questioning your coping mechanism.

It is there or they are there to make you believe that you're more okay than you are.

When you question them you undo the work that they spent so long on.

Sometimes you
don't think you
need to be held up,

sometimes you
just need someone
holding your hand
to remind you that
you can stand on
your own.

Although it wasn't true, you made me believe that my body was worth looking at.

That's a skill that not enough people give you credit for.

- *Honey*

I didn't want to be
alone.

I just didn't want to
be with anyone but you.

Perfect solitude

There was always someone waiting. Just like my dog waits for me to get home after a long day. Like a bucket waits to overflow and a spider waits to trap a fly.

You were waiting for me, when I was waiting for you.

You were speaking in
a language I didn't
understand at first,

but you taught me
how to be fluent.

I started relying
on a person,

and people are
not permanent.

Your notification used to be the only one that made me light up. I loved it. I started believing that because I was smiling I was happy.

Don't start relying on one source of happiness.

Like a wall,
if too many people
lean against it
the cement begins
to falter.

Just like your
saviour's smile.

You're human too,
but I overlooked
your struggles
because I couldn't
control my own.

I was so used
to dealing with
other people's
issues,

when you opened
up your sealed
can of secrets,

I simply forgot my
own.

The therapy friend

You were like a drug.

Cocaine.

When you weren't around,
I had withdrawal symptoms.

I looked over at the side of the bed that had now become eerily empty.

Two tears fell, one for you and one for me.

I dug my fingers into your shoulders searching for an answer that I knew you couldn't give me.

but I had convinced myself you could.

The smile tugging at my cheeks and the tears welling in my eyes confuse me sometimes.

How could anything be wrong? When you can still put a smile on my face.

I'm okay

Thank you, for what you ended up doing for me.

The way you cared, loved and made me feel like I wasn't alone.

But I drowned you out as you did, because you dealt with my problems before you even thought about your own.

I love that you helped me and I wouldn't ask for anything less, you pushed me on to my feet and got me walking again.

But now you're watching me from the floor, and I can't walk if you're not holding my hand.

How can you make me feel like I'm surrounded by everyone who loves me,

But I can't even make you feel like you have one person who cares.

- The moment I realised you were more human than I gave you credit for.

The accepting.

- There isn't anywhere you can run, and that's okay.

- We weren't meant to run from something that is built to follow.

There is something wrong.

But I know that now.

Running from something that was created to follow is impossible.

So why are you trying?

You can only ever be all in when it comes to yourself, because the only person you're ever going to lose and need to find again is yourself.

Of course I still get bad days, like everyone else, some days are rougher than others, and if you consider every day to be bad, then some days are even worse than every day.

The day I realised
that I only had
myself,
was the day I
realised only
I could save myself.

Sometimes.

Life takes a lot more.

Than just smiling through
the pain.

You'll know people, you'll leave people, you'll love people and you'll forget people, and as sour as it is to sit everyday knowing that you could still have that person, or you could still love that person, I think these things happen for a reason.

Bittersweet.

Is the best way to describe it.

Never tell your mother
you hate her.

You'll regret it in time.

Trust in yourself just like you trusted in the person who held your heart before they dropped it.

Staring at your ceiling for hours
is not very productive,

but there are some
pretty shapes up there.

Don't confuse accepting with fixing.

You must accept you're a little broken before you can fix it.

Why would you fix a mirror if you don't think it's cracked?

Some people are meant to tear you down, so you can build the strength to build yourself back up again.

Next time you'll be strong enough to stay standing.

All the glue in the world
may not be able to hold you together,

but that's because you're fabric
and you're using the wrong medium.

Just like losing weight,
healing also takes a lot longer
then you're willing to work for.

Just because you don't want to bother them,
or the thought of it is driving your over
thinking mad,

doesn't mean they aren't there.

You're not going to lose your mind only once, repetition is key to learning.

If someone has
ever told you
that your mental
health is fine
because your grades
are high,

I apologise that
whoever told you
does not
understand your
perseverance.

Yes, these lives we live are hard,
but they aren't impossible.

Some of us are just trained to
be stronger than others.

Because I couldn't get
rid of you if I tried,

make yourself
at home, there's
tea brewing.

The things that come and go in life aren't fair,
as a whole, they aren't.

I write like it's in the past, but I cannot deny that I suffer today.

You will always suffer somehow.

Physically or mentally, or both at the same time.

Whether it's as small as poor eyesight, or as large as paralysis.

Goodbyes are sour,
but we need them.

If we never had
to say goodbye,

We simply wouldn't
be real.

Once you come
out of your
little hiding hole,

you begin to
notice that
you're fragile,

because you
haven't been
experiencing the
world,

whilst you were
too worried
about your own
planet.

give yourself time to adjust.

Darling,
you cannot see
where you are going
if you aren't wearing
your glasses,

and you cannot find
them if the light is
off.

Your body,
will never look
exactly how you
want it to,

because mirrors
lie.

Loving yourself is like loving a ghost, possible, but most of the time very difficult.

I was walking
home on
a rainy day,

today in fact

and I thought,

How boring
would life be
without the rain?

As much as us Brits hate it, without it, the world would be so plain and not as green as we like it.

Apparently nothing comes to us that we like without something we don't first.

You seem to have fallen down a rabbit hole my love,

but you are not Alice,

so don't be down there too long.

When you are moving through hell, you cannot stop moving, or your feet will burn.

Stopping gets you nowhere, as I have learnt the hard way.

I won't apologise for all the bad things I felt and are yet to feel. Maybe in the future I may regret my choice of how I chose to live these past few years, but I know in this moment, I need to let my emotions run their course.

I'm not saying you can't be fragile,
I'm saying bring plasters.

You're never going to be 100% emotionally and physically at the same time, but that's what makes you human.

The living.

- You are still living when you feel like you're not.

- You cannot let a shadow out if there is no sunshine.

- Besides, the glow looks stunning on you.

The moment when
the first genuine
smile came through,

that was when I
realised,

nothing is
truly permanent.

Sing songs
to yourself,

laugh with
yourself,

dance with
yourself,

because although it may seem lonely, you are
your truest best friend, and you owe yourself a
bit of fun for everything you do for you.

The thing I love about life,
is that every day is
slightly different.

Smile at someone as
you walk past them,
send that person
a text.

Make their day
slightly different.

Find someone who is
just like you,

but in a different
font.

You'll get along
just fine,

trust me.

- *Honey*

Yes, these lives we live are hard,
and that's the fun part.

I like a good challenge.

Keep listening to music by yourself in your bedroom, keep humming the tune as it plays, because eventually, without realizing, you may hum yourself to the answer you want.

You can enjoy
the sunshine
from inside
too you
know.

Dolce far niente.

The Italian phrase
for the sweetness
of doing
nothing.

Find pleasure
in your
nothingness,
and you'll be
just fine.

Did you hear about that really great farmer?

He was outstanding in his field.

There's that smile.

Although, you're meant to be challenged, you are meant to have every single inconvenience and problem thrown at you, because you can't just float over the top of the mountain.

Water, go and drink some.

If you spend most of your time in your head, can I suggest planting some flowers, opening a few windows?

I don't want to remove you from your safe space, because you may thrive there perfectly.

I just want you to be comfortable.

Don't fall into the trap that being in love is a bad thing. Love is beautiful and strong, it creates clouds and birds and things we are yet to understand.

The problem is when you become so bitter over someone, you mistake everyone for them.

Live like your life
depends on
it,

because it
does.

Wear caution tape around your heart, for you do not want to attract anyone who isn't daring enough to have you.

You're worth more than you think.

When you
start romanticising
your life,

is when you
really start
living.

Once I went from labelling myself a hopeless romantic to a not so hopeless one, is when I may have discovered that not everything is as hopeless as I believed.

- A not so hopeless romantic.

Plot twist,
life is a game of chess
and it's your move.

You can call it suffering, like I regularly do, or you can take the time to call it battling.

It will punch and it will kick, but you can fight back, and harder than it does.

As much as I want to make this chapter longer I cannot. It's not because I'm not in a better place now or that I simply don't care about living. It's because I am still young, and although I want to believe that I can live like anyone older than me can, I have lived but not like I want to yet.

I haven't been to Australia, or watched the sunset and sunrise in one sitting. I haven't been swimming with dolphins and I haven't been to Disney world.

So what's the point of documenting about a lifetime I haven't finished yet.

There will be more. Always.

You're here finally, I've been waiting patiently. *How do you feel? Did you drink enough today? Eat enough?*

You've made it through the garden which is my mind, I spent a long time here, planting new colours and watering old ones. Some of them die, some live, but the ones that pass make room for new ones.

It's a heavy place to be, here, so thank you for making it through. Thank you for taking the time to embrace my insecurities whilst you embrace your own.

Being so young means that you've only experienced the beginning of me, my good parts and my worst. The bits I didn't think I would share, and the ones which everyone already knew.

Stretch out, breathe and relax.

We worked hard to be here, give yourself some credit.

I'm proud of you.

It's scary your mind.

You can't see or touch it and in most cases that can be frightening, but it's definitely there. It's that little voice which is reading this to you, it's holding your body together, and keeping this book in your hands.

But just like you're scared of it sometimes, it is scared of the world. It is you in a different form and it is only here for you.

Without it, you wouldn't be able to live through my life with me, or even live through your own.

Yes, it causes heartbreak, hurt and horrible experiences but it also heals them all eventually. It really is your best friend and your worst enemy, alongside motivation and time.

Right now, it may be your worst enemy, but give it the time to apologise, because it is only you, and *we are only human.*

Printed in Great Britain
by Amazon